008137603

821.91408 MCG

D0832804

You Tell Me

You Tell Me

Poems by
Roger McGough
and Michael Rosen

ILLUSTRATED BY
SARA MIDDA

KESTREL BOOKS

KESTREL BOOKS
Published by Penguin Books Ltd
Harmondsworth, Middlesex, England

Michael Rosen poems copyright © 1979 by Michael Rosen
Roger McGough poems copyright © 1969, 1971, 1973,
1974, 1976 and 1979 by Roger McGough
This collection copyright © 1979 by Penguin Books Ltd
Illustrations copyright © 1979 by Sara Midda

*The Acknowledgements on page 7 constitute an extension of
this copyright page.*

First published in 1979

ISBN 0 7226 5548 7

Printed in Great Britain by
Lowe & Brydone Printers Ltd, Thetford, Norfolk

Contents

Acknowledgements

For the following poems by Roger McGough acknowledgement is due to Jonathan Cape Ltd: 'The Fight of the Year' and 'Snipers' from *Watchwords*, © 1969 by Roger McGough; 'P.C. Plod and the Dale St Dogstrangler', 'Noodle Bug', 'Bucket' and 'Railings' from *After the Merrymaking*, © 1971 by Roger McGough; 'George and the Dragonfly' from *Gig*, © 1973 by Roger McGough; 'A Good Poem', 'Nooligan', 'Streemin', 'The Lesson', 'Bestlooking Girl', 'Footy Poem' and 'First Day at School' from *In the Glassroom*, © 1976 by Roger McGough.

For the following poems by Roger McGough acknowledgement is due to Eyre Methuen Ltd: 'Cousin Nell', 'Cousin Fosbury' and 'Cousin Reggie' from *Sporting Relations*, © 1974 by Roger McGough.

Roger McGough
and Michael Rosen

A Good Poem

I like a good poem
one with lots of fighting
in it. Blood, and the
clanging of armour.   Poems

against Scotland are good,
and poems that defeat
the French with crossbows.
I don't like poems that

aren't about anything.
Sonnets are wet and
a waste of time.
Also poems that don't

know how to rhyme.
If I was a poem
I'd play football and
get picked for England.

RMcG

You Tell Me

Here are the football results:
League Division Fun
Manchester United won, Manchester City lost.
Crystal Palace 2, Buckingham Palace 1
Millwall Leeds nowhere
Wolves 8 A cheese roll and had a cup of tea 2
Aldershot 3 Buffalo Bill shot 2
Evertonill, Liverpool's not very well either
Newcastle's Heaven Sunderland's a very nice place 2
Ipswhich one? You tell me.

                                                    MR

What's Your Name?

When they said
'What's your name?'
I used to say,
'Michael Rosen
Rosen
R,O,S,E,N
with a silent "Q" as in rhubarb.'

and they'd say,
'That's not very funny.

MR

P.C. Plod versus
the Dale St Dogstrangler

For several months
Liverpool was held in the grip of fear
by a dogstrangler most devilish,
who roamed the streets after dark
looking for strays. Finding one
he would tickle it seductively
about the body to gain its confidence,
then lead it down a deserted backstreet
where he would strangle the poor brute.
Hardly a night passed without somebody's
faithful fourlegged friend being dispatched
to that Golden Kennel in the sky.

The public were warned:
At the very first sign
of anything suspicious,
ring Canine-nine-nine.

Nine o'clock on the evening of January 11th
sees P.C. Plod on the corner
of Dale St and Sir Thomas St
disguised as a Welsh collie.
It is part of a daring plan to apprehend the strangler.
For though it is a wet and moonless night,
Plod is cheered in the knowledge
that the whole of the Liverpool City Constabulary
is on the beat that night disguised as dogs.

Not ten minutes earlier, a pekinese
(Policewoman Hodges)
had scampered past on her way to Clayton Square.

For Plod, the night passed uneventfully
and so in the morning he was horrified to learn
that no less than fourteen policemen and policewomen
had been tickled and strangled during the night.

The public were horrified
The Commissioner aghast
Something had to be done
And fast.

P.C. Plod (wise as a brace of owls)
met the challenge magnificently
and submitted an idea so startling in its vision
so audacious in its conception
that the Commissioner gasped
before ordering all dogs in the city
to be thereinafter disguised as fuzz.
The plan worked
and the dogstrangler was heard of no more.

Cops and mongrels
like P.C.s in a pod
To a grateful public
Plod was God.

So next time you're up in Liverpool
take a closer look
at that policeman on pointduty,
he might will be a copper spaniel.

RMcG

Rodge said,
'Teachers – they want it all ways –
You're jumping up and down on a chair
or something
and they grab hold of you and say,
"Would you do that sort of thing in your own home?"

'So you say, "No."
And they say,
"Well don't do it here then."

'But if you say, "Yes, I do it at home."
they say,
"Well, we don't want that sort of thing
going on here
thank you very much."

'Teachers – they get you all ways,'
Rodge said.

MR

When we go over
to my grandads
he falls asleep.

While he's asleep
he snores.

When he wakes up,
he says,
'Did I snore?
did I snore?
did I snore?'

Everybody says, 'No,
you didn't snore.'

Why do we lie to him?

MR

SNORE SNORE SNORE SNORE SNORE SNORE SNORE SNORE SNORE

The Lesson

A poem that raises the question:
Should there be capital punishment in schools?

Chaos ruled OK in the classroom
as bravely the teacher walked in
the nooligans ignored him
his voice was lost in the din

'The theme for today is violence
and homework will be set
I'm going to teach you a lesson
one that you'll never forget'

He picked on a boy who was shouting
and throttled him then and there
then garrotted the girl behind him
(the one with grotty hair)

Then sword in hand he hacked his way
between the chattering rows
'First come, first severed' he declared
'fingers, feet, or toes'

He threw the sword at a latecomer
it struck with deadly aim
then pulling out a shotgun
he continued with his game

The first blast cleared the backrow
(where those who skive hang out)
they collapsed like rubber dinghies
when the plug's pulled out

'Please may I leave the room sir?'
a trembling vandal enquired
'Of course you may' said teacher
put the gun to his temple and fired

The Head popped a head round the doorway
to see why a din was being made
nodded understandingly
then tossed in a grenade

And when the ammo was well spent
with blood on every chair
Silence shuffled forward
with its hands up in the air

The teacher surveyed the carnage
the dying and the dead
He waggled a finger severely
'Now let that be a lesson' he said

RMcG

Chivvy

Grown-ups say things like:
Speak up.
Don't talk with your mouth full
Don't stare
Don't point
Don't pick your nose
Sit up
Say please
Less noise
Shut the door behind you
Don't drag your feet
Haven't you got a hankie?

Take your hands out of your pockets
Pull your socks up
Stand up straight
Say thank you
Don't interrupt
No one thinks you're funny
Take your elbows off the table

Can't you make your *own*
mind up about anything?

MR

□

Some people
are always passing comments.
They say to me:
hallo hairy
your hands are huge
do you know your eyes pop out?
you're a monster
you aren't half white
your fingers are like sausages
you walk like a bear
is that thing on your chin a wart?

MR

Nooligan

I'm a nooligan
dont give a toss
in our class
I'm the boss
(well, one of them)

I'm a nooligan
got a nard 'ead
step out of line
and youre dead
(well, bleedin)

I'm a nooligan
I spray me name
all over town
footballs me game
(well, watchin)

I'm a nooligan
violence is fun
gonna be a nassassin
or a nired gun
(well, a soldier)

RMcG

Streemin

Im in the botom streme
Which meens Im not brigth
dont like reading
cant hardly write

but all these divishns
arnt reely fair
look at the cemtery
no streemin there

RMcG

☐

Mart was my best friend.
I thought he was great,
but one day he tried to do for me.

I had a hat – a woolly one
and I loved that hat.
It was warm and tight.
My mum had knitted it
and I wore it everywhere.

One day me and Mart were out
and we were standing at a bus-stop
and suddenly
he goes and grabs my hat
and chucked it over the wall.
He thought I was going to go in there
and get it out.
He thought he'd make me do that
because he knew I liked that hat so much
I wouldn't be able to stand being without it.

He was right –
I could hardly bear it.
I was really scared I'd never get it back.
But I never let on.
I never showed it on my face.
I just waited.

'Aren't you going to get your hat?'
he says.
'Your hat's gone,' he says.
'Your hat's over the wall.'
I looked the other way.

But I could still feel on my head
how he had pulled it off.
'Your hat's over the wall,' he says.
I didn't say a thing.

Then the bus came round the corner
at the end of the road.

If I go home without my hat
I'm going to walk through the door
and mum's going to say,
'Where's your hat?'
and if I say,
'It's over the wall,'
she's going to say,
'What's it doing there?'
and I'm going to say,
'Mart chucked it over,'
and she's going to say,
'Why didn't you go for it?'
and what am I going to say then?
what am I going to say then?

The bus was coming up.
'Aren't you going over for your hat?
There won't be another bus for ages,'
Mart says.

The bus was coming closer.
'You've lost your hat now,'
Mart says.

The bus stopped.
I got on
Mart got on
The bus moved off.

'You've lost your hat,' Mart says.

'You've lost your hat,' Mart says.

Two stops ahead, was ours.
'Are you going indoors without it?' Mart says.
I didn't say a thing.

The bus stopped.

Mart got up
and dashed downstairs.
He'd got off one stop early.
I got off when we got to our stop.

I went home
walked through the door
'Where's your hat?' Mum says.
'Over a wall,' I said.
'What's it doing there?' she says.
'Mart chucked it over there,' I said.
'But you haven't left it there, have you?' she says.
'Yes,' I said.

'Well don't you ever come asking me to make you
anything like that again.
You make me tired, you do.'

Later,
I was drinking some orange juice.
The front door-bell rang.
It was Mart.
He had the hat in his hand.
He handed it me – and went.

I shut the front door –
put on the hat
and walked into the kitchen.
Mum looked up.
'You don't need to wear your hat indoors do you?'
she said.
'I will for a bit,' I said.
And I did.

MR

Mart's advice:
If someone's acting big with you,
if someone's bossing you about
look very hard at one of their ears.
Keep your eyes fixed on it.
Don't let up.
Stare at it as if it was
a mouldy apple.
Keep staring.
Don't blink.

After a bit
you'll see their hand
go creeping up to touch it.
They're saying to themselves
'What's wrong with my ear?'

At that moment
you know you've won.

Smile.

MR

31

A Bad Habit

'Cigarette, Mike?' they say,
'I don't smoke,' I say.
'Haven't you got any bad habits?' they say,
'Yes,' I say, 'I chew bus tickets.'

I can't stop it.
The conductor gives me my ticket
and before I know I've done it
I've rolled it up
and I'm sucking on it like a cigarette.

I hold it with my fingers.
I roll it.
I flick it.
I hold it in my lips.

But there's a snag with my bus-ticket cigarettes:
they go soggy,
they go gooey
and I nibble
and I bite
and I chew –
my bus tickets get shorter and shorter
and before I know I've done it
all I've got is a ball of soggy paper
rolling round my mouth.

Disgusting.

Smokers buy pills to stop their filthy habit.
All I've got is bus inspectors.

You see, once, not long ago,
I was on a bus
and my ticket was in a ball
rolling round my mouth
and suddenly – above me –
there's the inspector.
'Tickets, please,' he says,
and there's me – nibble, nibble, nibble
on the mushed up ball of paper in my mouth.

He wants to see my ticket.
Of course he can see my ticket
if he doesn't mind inspecting
a little ball of mush.

So I say, 'Yes, you can see my ticket,'
and I stuck my finger in my mouth
and hauled out the blob.

He looks at it.
He looks at me.
It's sitting there on the end of my finger.
'What's that?' he says,
'My ticket,' I said,
'What did you have for breakfast?' he says,
'Corn Flakes,' I said.
'Mmm,' he says,
'Did you ever think of having a slice or two of toast,
as well, old son,' he says,
'and maybe you won't be so tempted by our tickets.'
And he left it at that.

But it's very hard to break the habit,
even after a warning like that.
Got any ideas?   MR

Snipers

When I was kneehigh to a tabletop,
Uncle Tom came home from Burma.
He was the youngest of seven brothers
so the street borrowed extra bunting
and whitewashed him a welcome.

All the relations made the pilgrimage,
including us, laughed, sang, made a fuss.
He was as brown as a chairleg,
drank tea out of a white mug the size of my head,
and said next to nowt.

But every few minutes he would scan
the ceiling nervously, hands begin to shake.
'For snipers,' everyone later agreed,
'A difficult habit to break.'

Sometimes when the two of us were alone,
he'd have a snooze after dinner
and I'd keep an eye open for Japs.
Of course, he didn't know this
and the tanner he'd give me before I went
was for keeping quiet,
but I liked to think it was money well spent.

Being Uncle Tom's secret bodyguard
had its advantages, the pay was good
and the hours were short, but even so,
the novelty soon wore off, and instead,
I started school and became an infant.

Later, I learned that he was in a mental home.
'Needn't tell anybody . . . Nothing serious
. . . Delayed shock . . . Usual sort of thing
. . . Completely cured now the doctors say.'
The snipers came down from the ceiling
but they didn't go away.

Over the next five years they picked off
three of his brothers; one of whom was my father.
No glory, no citations,
Bang! straight through the heart.

Uncle Tom's married now, with a family.
He doesn't say much, but each night after tea,
he still dozes fitfully in his favourite armchair,
(dreams by courtesy of Henri Rousseau).
He keeps out of the sun, and listens now and then
for the tramp tramp tramp of the Colonel Bogeymen.
He knows damn well he's still at war,
just that the snipers aren't Japs anymore.

RMcG

Busy Day

Pop in
pop out
pop over the road
pop out for a walk
pop in for a talk
pop down to the shop
can't stop
got to pop

got to pop?

pop where?
pop what?

well
I've got to
pop round
pop up
pop in to town
pop out and see
pop in for tea
pop down to the shop
can't stop
got to pop

got to pop?

pop where?
pop what?

well
I've got to
pop in
pop out
pop over the road
pop out for a walk
pop in for a talk . . . .

MR

THE HARDEST THING TO DO
IN THE WORLD
is stand in the hot sun
at the end of a long queue for ice creams
watching all the people who've just bought theirs
coming away from the queue
giving their ice creams their very first lick.

MR

Olympic Special

'It's Olympic Special!'

'And now over to David Coleman
for the start
of the 4 × 100 metres relay heats.'

'Welcome back to the Athletics Stadium
for the 4 × 100 metres relay.
The British Team are in Lane One
and first to run is Hauck . . .'

Hauck. Mick Hauck.
He punched me in the corridor.
I mean he punched me in the belly
in the corridor.
I got him in a headlock
over the knee
on the ground
knee on the chest
and then –
well . . . then to the head's office.

While we were waiting outside the office
he said, 'Look Rosie,
the head'll say, "What do you think you were doing?"
then he'll say, "Why?" – He always says, "Why?"
Say, you don't know. You were being stupid.'

We go in
The head says to Mick Hauck
'What do you think you were doing?'
'I don't know, sir.' Mick Hauck says.
He turns to me.
'Why were you fighting?' he says.
'I was being stupid, sir,' I say.
'You're telling me,' he says.
'Can't you stop being stupid?' he says.
'No sir,' says Mick Hauck.
'For godssake just try, will you,' he says . . .

'. . . and they're under starter's orders
and they're OFF
Hauck is holding well against Badenski in Lane 2 . . .'

Outside his office
Hauck said, 'I always tell him I was being stupid,
because that's what *he* thinks.
Then he can't think of anything else to say, can he?'

MR

40

Down behind the dustbin
I met a dog called Ted.
'Leave me alone,' he says,
'I'm just going to bed.'

Down behind the dustbin
I met a dog called Felicity.
'It's a bit dark here,' she said,
'They've cut off the electricity.'

Down behind the dustbin
I met a dog called Roger.
'Do you own this bin?' I said.
'No. I'm only the lodger.'

Ian said,
Down behind the dustbin
I met a dog called Sue.
'What are you doing here?' I said.
'I've got nothing else to do.'

Down behind the dustbin
I met a dog called Anne.
'I'm just off now,' she said,
'to see a dog about a man.'

Down behind the dustbin
I met a dog called Jack.
'Are you going anywhere?' I said.
'No. I'm just coming back.'

Down behind the dustbin
I met a dog called Billy.
'I'm not talking to you,' I said,
'if you're going to be silly.'

Down behind the dustbin
I met a dog called Barry.
He tried to take the bin away
but it was too heavy to carry.

Down behind the dustbin
I met a dog called Mary.
'I wish I wasn't a dog,' she said,
'I wish I was a canary.'

MR

Three Tongue Twisters

If he could sell her salt,
I could sell her a salt-cellar
for salt for her celery

I watched a Car-Wash wash a car
I wish I was washed like Car-Washes wash cars

She said
should she show a soldier
her shoulder?

MR

One day when I was young
there was going to be a fancy dress show.
For a while I couldn't think
who to go as.
I didn't have any cowboy hats
or moustaches or angel's wings.
I couldn't think what to go as.

Then I suddenly thought,
'I could go as My Mum'
I could get up in an old skirt of hers,
hat and coat –
and there I'd be – My Mum.

Mum thought it was a really good idea
and she gave me her old green skirt
she didn't wear anymore
and a horrible fawn coat-jacket thing
with big shoulders and gold buttons.
I wore shorts underneath the skirt
no socks, just sandals
and I put on a straw hat
and mum found me an old black shiny handbag.
Dressed up like that I now had to get to the hall
where the show was on.

I waited till it was dark
and then I ran through the streets
holding the skirt up round my knees.

When I got there, it had already begun.
And I couldn't quite understand
what was going on,
because, you see, all the rest of the children
were standing around in the hall very very still,
and the woman in charge was going round
putting her face very close to the children's faces
and trying to make them laugh.

So there was Richard Russell
who had a beard, a black shirt
a pair of his sister's tights on
and one of those white frilly things
you put round birthday cakes –
he had round his neck
and the woman was right up against his nose
and saying in a very high voice:
'Hallo Willy. Willy Willy Shakespeare.
Have you written a play today, Willy?'

Someone said I had to go and stand out there
and I wasn't to laugh
and I'd win.
So I went out there
and she went on round the hall
talking in this very high voice:
'Hallo Big Ears.
Where's Noddy?
Beep, beep in his little car is he?'
And they were creasing up in giggles
all over the place.

Then she got to me.
And she said,
'Who are you?' she said,
'My Mum,' I said.
And everyone in the hall laughed.
They laughed and laughed.
At first I thought they were laughing
because I had made a good joke
and then I saw that they were laughing
because they thought I was stupid.
That annoyed me.

So this woman who had also laughed at me,
now tried to make me laugh
by putting her big puffy red face close to mine
and saying,
'Are you My Mum? Oh you are looking nice today,
    mummy.'
Well obviously I didn't think that was very funny –
in fact I thought it was pathetic.
But she kept at it.
'Hallo Mummy. Mummy can I have some sweets
    please?'

So I didn't laugh.
But the others did.
But I didn't win though.
I think Big Ears won.
He got a box of chocolates and a pack of cards.
Then we all went home.

As we were walking down the road
away from the place,
a boy called Terence,
who wasn't allowed to play with me
because his mum said I was common,
he said, 'You're daft, you are.
Why did you come dressed up as your mother?
You wouldn't find your mother in Madame Tussaud's
    Waxworks,
would you?'

When I got in,
I asked mum what a Waxworks was.
She told me how it was a place
where they make big life-size wax dolls
of famous people.
Then I said, 'I didn't win mum,
because you're not famous enough to be a waxwork.'
'Oh well, never mind,' she says,
'we can't all be famous can we?' she says,
and I said, 'But no – don't you see –
I didn't laugh. I should've won. I didn't laugh.'

MR

I was sitting in the sitting room
toying with some toys
when from a door marked: 'GRUESOME'
There came a GRUESOME noise.

Cautiously I opened it
and there to my surprise
a little GRUE lay sitting
with tears in its eyes

'Oh little GRUE please tell me
what is it ails thee so?'
'Well I'm so small,' he sobbed,
'GRUESSES don't want to know'

'Exercises are the answer,
Each morning you must DO SOME'
He thanked me, smiled,
and do you know what?
The very next day he . . .

McG

A long time ago
there was a man who lived round our way
and he said:
'When I die,
I don't want to be buried in the ground
I want to be buried in the air.'
So he set about making sure
he would be buried in the air.
He got people to build him a big yellow tower.
He said, 'I want to be buried halfway up this tower.'
Not long after, he died.
When they came to bury him
they decided that they didn't want to bury him
in the air, halfway up the tower,
so they buried him in the ground instead
and there was nothing on earth he could do about it.
But the tower's still there
and everyone knows it was built for the man
who wanted to be buried in the air
but couldn't make sure he would be.

MR

Noodle Bug

One bright Thursday morning
P.C. Plod was on pointduty in Williamson Square
when he was approached by an oriental gentleman,
new to the city, who wanted to know
the whereabouts of a certain Chinese restaurant.
To Plod, one Chinese restaurant was as good,
or as bad, as another, and so he
directed the old man to the nearest.

Ten minutes later, the old man returned:
'Please could you dilect me to Yuet Ben Lestaurant'
'That's a coincidence' remarked Plod
'You're the second Chinaman to ask me that
in ten minutes, is there a party on?'
'Me same Chinaman,' explained the same Chinaman.
To cover up his embarrassment,
Plod gave detailed directions
of a restaurant on the far side of the city.
The old man trundled off.

Twenty minutes later, tired and angry,
he was back in Williamson Square.
Lest a member of our Police Force be thought
less than wonderful and idiotic to boot,
Plod sought immediately to pacify
the stranger with polite conversation.
'Now then sir what have you there in that large bag
that weighs so heavily upon you?'
'In bag there is special Chinese flour'
'And what's that used for sir?'
persisted the trafficontrolling seeker
of eternal truth and wisdom.

'Ah well, special flour is mixed with water until
velly soft and then whole family arrive for
ceremony and everybody pull and roll and pull
and roll and pull and roll until we have big soft
noodle six foot in length'
'Garn, silliest thing I ever heard' scoffed Plod
'What could you do with a big soft noodle six foot long?'
'You could put it on pointduty in Williamson Square'
suggested the old man and

ran

off

down

the

Fork Week

You're going to lay the table.
You go to the drawer to get the knives, forks and
	spoons.
You find the forks
You find the spoons
but the knives – they've all gone.
You look everywhere
the sink, the table, the draining board
but they've all gone.

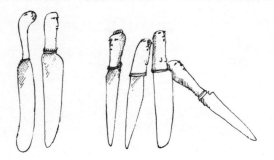

A few days later – it's the same
only it's the spoons this time
and all the knives have come back.

My brother,
he's worked it out,
he says they take it in turns to disappear.
'It's alright,' he says,
'We won't see another fork till Thursday,
it's Fork Week.'

MR

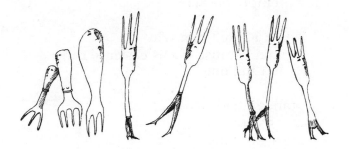

Bucket

every evening after tea
grandad would take his bucket for a walk

An empty bucket

When i asked him why
he said because it was easier to carry
than a full one

grandad had
an answer
for everything

RMcG

Railings

towards the end of his tether
grandad
at the drop of a hat
would paint the railings

overnight
we became famous
allover the neighbourhood
for our smart railings

(and our dirty hats)

RMcG

Bestlooking Girl

Im the bestlooking girl in our year
It's a fact

All the lads fancy me, and the girls
Are jealous

Mind you, all the lads here are rubbish
Just like kids

My boyfriend is a deejay in town
In a club

He sounds american but he's not
He's scottish

He wants to get on Radio One
Then TV

He thinks I'm 16 so I let him
Now and then

RMcG

Footy Poem

I'm an ordinary feller 6 days of the week
But Saturday turn into a football freak.
I'm a schizofanatic, sad but it's true
One half of me's red, and the other half's blue.

I can't make me mind up which team to support
Whether to lean to starboard or port
I'd be bisexual if I had time for sex
Cos it's Goodison one week and Anfield the next.

But the worst time of all is Derby day
One half of me's at home and the other's away
So I get down there early all ready for battle
With me rainbow scarf and me two-tone rattle.

And I'm shouting for Latchford and I'm shouting for
      Hughes
'Come on de Pool' – 'Gerrin dere Blues'
'Give it ter Heighway' – 'Worra puddin'
'King of der Kop' – All of a sudden – Wop!
'Goal!' – 'Offside!'

And after the match as I walk back alone
It's argue, argue all the way home
Some nights when I'm drunk I've even let fly
An give meself a poke in the eye

But in front of the fire watchin' 'Match of the Day'
Tired but happy, I look at it this way:
Part of me's lost and part of me's won
I've had twice the heartaches – but I've had twice the fun.

RMcG

Going Through the Old Photos

Who's that?
That's your Auntie Mabel
and that's me
under the table.

Who's that?
That's Uncle Billy.
Who's that?
Me being silly.

Who's that
licking a lolly?
I'm not sure
but I think it's Polly.

Who's that
behind the tree?
I don't know,
I can't see.
Could be you.
Could be me.

Who's that?
Baby Joe.
Who's that?
I don't know.

Who's that standing
on his head?
Turn it round.
It's Uncle Ted.

MR

scratch

I know a cat that scratched a baby.
It's prowling around the legs
of the baby's mother
looking for a stroke.

It's an animal.
Animals don't know
we don't stroke
people who hurt.

stroke stroke stroke stroke

Scram

It gets out
through the same window
it got in.
It'll scratch more babies.
It'll hunt more strokes
that cat I know.

MR

'The Fight of the Year'

'And there goes the bell for the third month
and Winter comes out of its corner looking groggy
Spring leads with a left to the head
followed by a sharp right to the body
    daffodils
    primroses
    crocuses
    snowdrops
    lilacs
    violets
    pussywillow
Winter can't take much more punishment
and Spring shows no signs of tiring
    tadpoles
    squirrels
    baalambs
    badgers
    bunny rabbits
    mad march hares
    horses and hounds
Spring is merciless
Winter won't go the full twelve rounds
    bobtail clouds
    scallywaggy winds
    the sun
    a pavement artist
    in every town
A left to the chin
and Winter's down!

tomatoes
radish
cucumber
onions
beetroot
celery
and any
amount
of lettuce
for dinner
Winter's out for the count
Spring is the winner!'

RMcG

FOR DINNER

Who's been at the toothpaste?
I know some of you do it right
and you squeeze the tube from the bottom
and you roll up the tube as it gets used up, don't you?

But somebody
somebody here –
you know who you are
you dig your thumb in
anywhere, anyhow
and you've turned that tube of toothpaste
into a squashed sock.
You've made it so hard to use
it's like trying to get toothpaste
out of a packet of nuts.

You know who you are.
I won't ask you to come out here now
but you know who you are.

And then you went and left the top off didn't you?
So the toothpaste turned to cement.

People who do things like that should . . .
you should be ashamed of yourself.

I am.

MR

□

A true story

First love
when I was ten.

We planned a trip
up to town
Quite a grand thing to do
Up to town
The long ride on the train
all the way
up to town.

The day before our trip
up to town
She said, 'Do you mind if Helen
comes with us
up to town?'
'Great,' I said,
'all three of us, we'll all go
on the train
up to town.'

So that's how it was –
all three of us,
her, Helen and me,
going on our trip
up to town.

But when we got
up to town,
all three of us –
her, Helen and me,

there was this long tunnel
and her friend, Helen,
goes and says:
'Hey – let's run away from him.'
And that's what they did.

So then there wasn't
all three of us any more.
There was just me,
standing in the tunnel.
I didn't chase after them.
I went home.

MR

First Day at School

A millionbillionwillion miles from home
Waiting for the bell to go. (To go where?)
Why are they all so big, other children?
So noisy? So much at home they
must have been born in uniform
Lived all their lives in playgrounds
Spent the years inventing games
that don't let me in. Games
that are rough, that swallow you up.

And the railings.
All around, the railings.
Are they to keep out wolves and monsters?
Things that carry off and eat children?
Things you don't take sweets from?
Perhaps they're to stop us getting out
Running away from the lessins. Lessin.
What does a lessin look like?
Sounds small and slimy.
They keep them in glassrooms.
Whole rooms made out of glass. Imagine.

I wish I could remember my name
Mummy said it would come in useful.
Like wellies. When there's puddles.
Lellowwellies. I wish she was here.
I think my name is sewn on somewhere
Perhaps the teacher will read it for me.
Tea-cher. The one who makes the tea.

RMcG

□

I used to have a little red alarm clock.
It was my dad's.
He gave me it
and I used to keep it by the side of my bed.

It was very small and it had legs
only the legs were like little balls –
little metal balls,
and you could unscrew them
out of the bottom of that little red clock.

One morning
I was lying in bed
and I was fiddling with my clock
and I unscrewed one of those
little ball-leg things
and, do you know what I did?
I slipped it into my mouth – to suck,
like a gob-stopper.

Well it was sitting there,
underneath my tongue
when I rolled over
and – ghulkh – I swallowed it:
the leg off my clock.
It had gone. It was inside me. A piece of metal.

I looked at the clock.
It was leaning over on its side.
I stood it up and of course it fell over.

So I got up,
went downstairs with it
and I was holding it out in front of me
and I walked in to the kitchen
and I said:
'Look, the clock. The leg. The leg. The clock – er . . .'

And my dad took it off me and he said,
'What's up, lad? Did you lose it?
Not to worry, it can't have gone far.
We'll find it,
and we can screw it back on here, look.'

'I swallowed it,' I said.

'You swallowed it? You swallowed it?
Are you mad? Are you stark staring mad?
You've ruined a perfectly good clock.
That was a good clock, that was. Idiot.
Now what's the use of a clock that won't stand up?'
He held it out in front of him,
and he stared at it. I looked at it too.
I was wondering what was happening to the leg.

MR

George and the Dragonfly

Georgie Jennings was spit almighty.
When the golly was good
he could down a dragonfly at 30 feet
and drown a 100 midges with the fallout.
At the drop of a cap
he would outspit lads
years older and twice his size.
Freckled and rather frail
he assumed the quiet dignity
beloved of schoolboy heroes.

But though a legend in his own playtime
Georgie Jennings failed miserably in the classroom
and left school at 15 to work for his father.
And talents such as spitting
are considered unbefitting
for upandcoming porkbutchers.

I haven't seen him since,
but like to imagine some summer soiree
when, after a day moistening mince,
George and his wife entertain tanned friends.
and after dinner, sherrytongued talk
drifts back to schooldays
The faces halfrecalled, the adventures
overexaggerated. And the next thing
that shy sharpshooter of days gone by
is led, vainly protesting, on to the lawn
where, in the hush of a golden august evening
a reputation, 20 years tall, is put to the test.

So he takes extra care as yesterheroes must,
fires, and a dragonfly, encapsulated, bites the dust.
Then amidst bravos and tinkled applause,
blushing, Georgie leads them back indoors.

RMcG

☐ ·

Cousin Nell
married a frogman
in the hope
that one day
he would turn into
a handsome prince.

Instead he turned into
a sewage pipe
near Gravesend
and was never seen again.

RMcG

Cousin Fosbury
took his highjumping seriously.
To ensure a floppier flop
he consulted a contortionist
and had his vertebrae removed
by a backstreet vertebraeortionist.

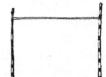

Now he clears 8 foot with ease
and sleeps with his head
tucked under his knees.

RMcG

Cousin Reggie
who adores the sea
lives in the Midlands
unfortunately.

He surfs down escalators
in department stores
and swims the High Street
on all of his fours.

Sunbathes on the pavement
paddles in the gutter
(I think our Reggie's
a bit of a nutter).   RMcG

71

When you're a GROWN-UP
a SERIOUS and SENSIBLE PERSON
When you've stopped being SILLY
you can go out and have babies
and go into a SERIOUS and SENSIBLE shop
and ask for:
Tuftytails, Paddipads, Bikkipegs, Cosytoes
and
Tommy Tippee Teethers.
Sno-bunnies, Visivents, Safeshines
Comfybaths, Dikkybibs
and
Babywipes.
Rumba Rattles and Trigger Jiggers
A Whirlee Three, a Finger Flip
or A Quacky Duck.
And if you're very SENSIBLE
you can choose
Easifitz, Babybuggies and a Safesitterstand.
Or is it a
Saferstandsit?
No it's a Sitstandsafe. I can never remember.
I'm sorry but Babytalk is a very difficult language.
It's for adults only.
Like 'X' films
Much too horrible for children.

MR

72